The Apostles' Creed

By Jim Gimbel

with Jo Gimbel, Abby Gimbel and Andy Gimbel

Illustrated by Susan Morris

CONCORDIA PUBLISHING HOUSE • SAINT LOUIS

This collection published
in 2006 by Concordia Publishing House
3558 S. Jefferson Avenue, St. Louis, MO 63118-3968
1-800-325-3040 • www.cph.org

Originally published as individual Arch® Books under the titles *God, My Creator,* copyright
© 2003 Concordia Publishing House, *Jesus, My Savior,* copyright © 2003 Concordia Publishing
House, and *Holy Spirit, My Helper,* copyright © 2004 Concordia Publishing House.

Manufactured in China

1 2 3 4 5 6 7 8 9 10   15 14 13 12 11 10 09 08 07 06

I believe in God, the Father

Almighty, Maker of heaven and earth.

And in Jesus Christ, His only Son, our Lord,

who was conceived by the Holy Spirit,

born of the Virgin Mary,

suffered under Pontius Pilate,

was crucified, died and was buried.

He descended into hell.

The third day He rose again from the dead.

He ascended into heaven

and sits at the right hand of God,

the Father Almighty.

From thence He will come to judge

the living and the dead.

I believe in the Holy Spirit,

the holy Catholic Church,

the communion of saints,

the forgiveness of sins,

the resurrection of the body,

and the life everlasting. Amen.

Dear Parent,

Thank you for sharing this book with your child. There is nothing more important to a child than knowing God. A child who knows the truth of him- or herself in relation to God begins to develop a foundation for answering some key human questions: Who am I? Where did I come from? What is the meaning and purpose of life? Is there more to life than what we know? What is most valuable in life? Where is God when life hurts? How is my life fulfilled?

Most likely, you have already shared the key message of God's love for the world through Jesus Christ when you've read or told Bible stories. Often children who hear the accounts of David and Goliath, Jonah, Daniel in the lions' den, or Peter walking on water easily relate them to the human characters. When the story is told in the right way, children see the characteristics of God in action through these events— what He is doing for our salvation. Bible stories tell us about God and His love for us despite our sinful human condition.

The pictures we get of God from Bible stories are like pieces of a puzzle. No single story sums up everything that God is or explains the basic core of what we believe about God. Children (and adults) need help to see the big picture. That is the value of the creeds. The historic Christian creeds briefly summarize and pull together the most basic and universal puzzle pieces to show us a picture of God.

This book is divided into three parts, just like the Apostles' Creed. One characteristic God reveals about Himself is that He is triune—three distinct persons in one divine being. They are all fully God, sharing divine characteristics, but each Person has different works ascribed to Him. The First Person, God the Creator, is our heavenly Father, attributed with creating and preserving everything we know in the world (including

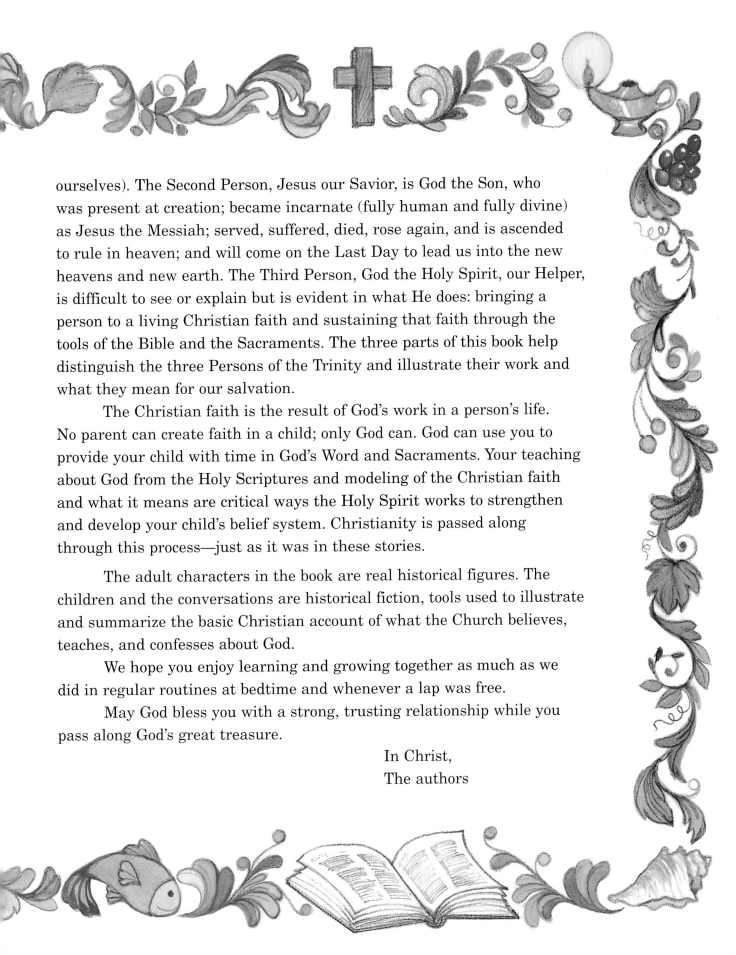

ourselves). The Second Person, Jesus our Savior, is God the Son, who was present at creation; became incarnate (fully human and fully divine) as Jesus the Messiah; served, suffered, died, rose again, and is ascended to rule in heaven; and will come on the Last Day to lead us into the new heavens and new earth. The Third Person, God the Holy Spirit, our Helper, is difficult to see or explain but is evident in what He does: bringing a person to a living Christian faith and sustaining that faith through the tools of the Bible and the Sacraments. The three parts of this book help distinguish the three Persons of the Trinity and illustrate their work and what they mean for our salvation.

The Christian faith is the result of God's work in a person's life. No parent can create faith in a child; only God can. God can use you to provide your child with time in God's Word and Sacraments. Your teaching about God from the Holy Scriptures and modeling of the Christian faith and what it means are critical ways the Holy Spirit works to strengthen and develop your child's belief system. Christianity is passed along through this process—just as it was in these stories.

The adult characters in the book are real historical figures. The children and the conversations are historical fiction, tools used to illustrate and summarize the basic Christian account of what the Church believes, teaches, and confesses about God.

We hope you enjoy learning and growing together as much as we did in regular routines at bedtime and whenever a lap was free.

May God bless you with a strong, trusting relationship while you pass along God's great treasure.

In Christ,
The authors

God, My Creator

Genesis 1–2; Psalm 103; Psalm 139:1–18;
and Psalm 145 for children

Explanation of the
FIRST ARTICLE
of the Apostles' Creed

Written by
Jim Gimbel, with Jo Gimbel

The apostle quit speaking; the crowd went away.
But 8-year-old Michael decided to stay.
He had lots of questions; his face was aglow.
This God-of-Three-Persons he wanted to know.

So Michael ran up to Bartholomew's side.
"Please teach me, I want to know more," the boy cried.
Bartholomew had a kind look on his face.
His smile and manner reflected God's grace.

"What can we say to show God's for real?
We can't see Him or hear Him—His hand we can't feel!
I believe," the boy said, "I'm baptized; I'm His own.
But how is it then that this God becomes known?"

Bartholomew thought for a minute, then said,
"You're wise, my young friend, to think with your head.
True believing involves both the head and the heart.
Also, loving and living set this faith apart."

Then Michael looked 'round and saw other gods too.
He asked, "Why do we say that just our God is true?"
Bartholomew gave a loud chuckle, "You see,
He's different and better than any of these!

"Those gods are just statues; they're not kind or good.
Their image is carved out of marble or wood.
They're not living or real; they can't help in our need.
They can't listen, no matter how long we might plead.

"Let's talk first of knowing the God we can't see.
His fingerprints mark every bush, every tree.
Each animal, too, whether big or quite small—
By the Word of His mouth, God created them all.

"He made Earth out of nothing. He spoke; it was so.
He made raindrops and hail and fluffy, white snow.
He made sun, moon, and stars that give off their light.
He keeps nature in balance, things that fall—things in flight.

"Then last, but not least, God made the first man
 To work and take care of it all was His plan.
 God made brains that could think and eyes that could see;
 He made every small part that together makes 'me.'

"He made us complete, with both body and soul
 So we'd live with Him always 'cause that was His goal.
 He also made angels to do what He says.
 Every bit of creation's most certainly His!

"Of millions of people no two are alike,
Each person is special like you, my dear Mike.
God gives families who love us, our moms and dads too,
Helped by teachers and leaders who guide our way through.

"God gives people homes; He provides them with clothes.
He gives fish, fruit, and vegetables, even bread loaves.
He gives all that we have; He gives all that we need.
He protects, He defends, and He truly will lead.

"But as great as He is with His power and all,
He loves us enough to hear when we call.
He's the best Father ever; He's firm and He's fair.
There's nothing so strong as His great, tender care.

"Though all was made perfect in only six days,
The first people did evil and went their own ways.
But our Father is loving and sent His own Son.
Through Jesus, the Savior, forgiveness was won.

"He wants us to trust Him with all of our heart
But even this act is His gift from the start.
He helps us be thankful and sing to His praise,
To serve and obey Him for all of our days."

Michael believed; his faith and trust grew.
The love of his heavenly Father was true.
When he went home that night, he had peace and true joy
Because he knew God the Father loved His little boy.

2

Jesus, My Savior

The Book of Luke and Acts 1 for children

Explanation of the
SECOND ARTICLE
of the Apostles' Creed

Written by Jim Gimbel,
with Abby Gimbel

The boys on the seashore were learning their trade.
They worked hard, they listened, and sometimes they played.
They were taught how to sail, clean a fish, mend a net.
They learned all day long from sunrise to sunset.

Their master was Clement, who had learned at this shore
From a fisher named Peter, who knew fish and more.
He taught all that he knew; fishing secrets he shared,
But he also taught Jesus, with whom none compared.

As the boys cleaned the fish and their chatter would run,
Clement told the great deeds of Jesus, God's Son,
Who was promised to Eve, to Abram and Ruth,
To all who would listen and hear of God's truth.

How God's Son, humbly born, though the King of creation,
Was the Savior of all, including God's nation;
Born of a virgin, sweet Mary, by name;
Pledged to Joseph, to whom angel Gabriel came.

With God His true Father and Mary His mother,
Full God and full man has no equal, no other.
He was human completely, but yet without sin.
He had all the God-powers, full of grace from within.

"Was He spirit alone in a body we see?"

"Was He just a great man God adopted, like me?"

"Did He switch between God and the man as He chose?"

"No, no, no," said Clement, like a teacher who knows.

Then the girl with a jar said, "I don't understand.
Is Jesus true God, or is Jesus true man?"
Said Clement, "He's both, in a way we can't see.
As true God, He forgives all; as true man, dies for me."

"So tell us some stories," the boys begged for more.
"Well," said Clement, "He once taught from this very shore.
He healed many, like lepers, fed folks fish and bread;
He calmed a great storm, water-walked, raised the dead.

"But of all the great things in His life that He did,
The best deed of all? When He died for us, kid!
Though He never did sin or commit any crime,
He was captured and tried before Pilate one time.

"He was hung on a cross, where He suffered and died,
While His followers watched from a distance and cried.
His body was buried in a borrowed new tomb;
His full person, dead briefly, was not held in gloom.

"He announced throughout hell that a victory He'd won;
He didn't stay dead; by His life, life's begun!
When He rose from the dead three days after the grave,
He revealed to believers His power to save.

"The good news for us, my dear friends, as you see,
  Is that through Jesus' death, He's redeemed you and me.
  Although we are lost and condemned by our sin,
  By Christ's death on the cross, resurrection *we* win!

"He buys us all back, as the Scriptures have told,
  But with His lifeblood, most precious, not silver or gold.
  Since the wages of sin have been taken away,
  We now can be with Him forever some day.

"Forty days after He rose from the dead,
  He went back to heaven, just as He said.
  He sits by the Father on a great and high throne
  Where He rules and He reigns and His name is well-known.

"From there He'll come back, though we do not know when.
  But He'll judge every person who's ever lived, then.
  And all who believe He's the Truth, Life, and Way—
  Their Redeemer and Savior—with Him they will stay.

"Now since we know that we are His own,
  We don't need to fear; we are never alone.
  He's defeated the devil; He's conquered our sin.
  Through His resurrection, even death cannot win."

The boys learned of Jesus from Clement each day.
  They lived for, served, loved Him, and often did say,
"I believe in this Jesus, my God who's the Word,
  He's most certainly, truly, my Savior and Lord."

3

Holy Spirit, My Helper

Matthew 28:19;
1 Corinthians 12:3;
Galatians 5:22–23;
Titus 3:5–7 for children

Explanation of the
THIRD ARTICLE
of the Apostles' Creed

Written by Jim Gimbel,
with Andy Gimbel

Young Lucas was rushing to finish his chores—
Trimming wicks, making beds, cutting wood, sweeping floors.
For the guests at the inn would expect these all done,
And, when finished, he'd work on his own, just for fun.

He was learning his letters—to read and to write.
Quite often he'd study till late in the night.
Since a wise and kind doctor he wanted to be,
He wrote, read, and learned of the human body.

Then a message was sent; an apostle was near.
He would stay at their inn; crowds would gather to hear.
So young Lucas prepared the best guest room upstairs.
The boy was excited; he rushed through his prayers.

Philip later arrived, settled in, ate a meal,
With the boy sitting near, taking notes in detail.
The believers then gathered and filled the dark room.
As they listened, each word brought new light, chased the gloom.

Since the believers who gathered all knew Christ the Lord
And were certain God made the whole world by His Word,
The focus for Philip was the great Holy Spirit.
Phil spoke boldly aloud so each person would hear it.

First, he taught how the world, plus the lies of the devil,
With our own wicked nature combine—triple evil.
These three powerful foes fight us right from our birth.
Since God's image is gone, we by rights have no worth.

"All the sins of the world—pride, deceit, and self-love—
Are well-known to the Lord of the heavens above.
Jesus paid for all sins when He died on the cross,
But for those who don't know Him, this act is a loss.

"Our minds are deceived; on our own, can't believe.
We are dead, closed to God, blind in heart, enemies.
We can't choose Him or see Him; our lives we can't fill.
We can't even please Him; we can't seek His will.

"We are blind, we are dead, and we fight against God
Till the Spirit breaks through, calls, and gives us the nod.
By the Gospel's great power Christ's gifts we receive.
By the Spirit alone we both know and believe.

"God daily and richly forgives all our sins.
Through His tools—Word and Water—our new life begins.
He's the great protector, this Spirit of love,
As He keeps us in Christ here on earth and above.

"The Spirit's main work, then, is sanctification.
Renewing, rebuilding us, His new creation.
He helps us to live by His Word and His way.
Though not perfect, we try as we think, do, and say.

"The Spirit unites all of those who believe.
We all are God's saints, who His graces receive.
His children He gathers like sheep in a fold.
They form churches together, the young and the old."

Lucas wrote down each point, noting every last word
From St. Philip, who'd seen God's great Spirit outpoured.
Luke then asked what the gifts of the Spirit might be?
Phil said, "Faith, hope, peace, joy, love that's giv'n freely.

"Though earth's treasures break down, rot, erode, start to rust,
Though we die and our bodies decay, turn to dust.
When our Savior returns, all the dead He will raise.
All believers will live to give eternal praise."

When young Lucas had written down every last word,
Said, "It's true that this Spirit—true God—is my Lord!"
Said St. Philip to Lucas, the doctor to be,
"By your writing they'll know of God's full Trinity."